ANIMAL ALPHABET

BERT KITCHEN

DIAL BOOKS

NEW YORK

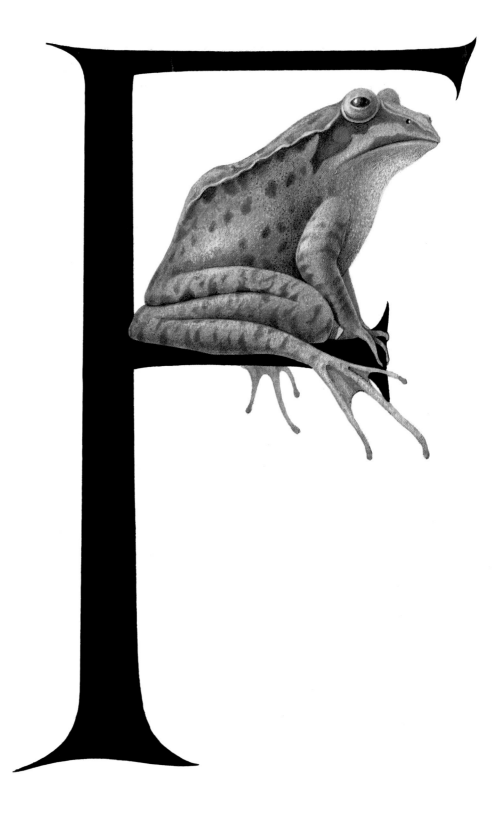

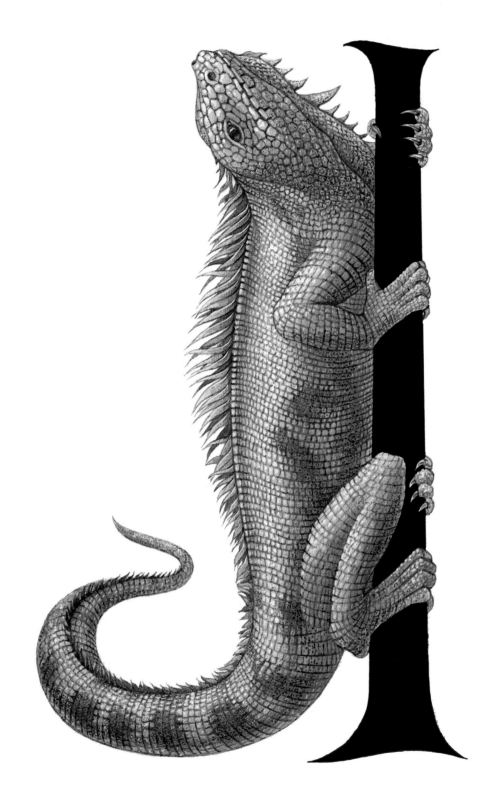

ANIMAL ANSWERS

A	Armadillo (Nine-banded)	**N**	Newt
B	Bat	**O**	Ostrich
C	Chameleon (Mediterranean)	**P**	Penguin (Rockhopper)
D	Dodo	**Q**	Quetzal
E	Elephant	**R**	Rhinoceros
F	Frog	**S**	Snail
G	Giraffe	**T**	Tortoise
H	Hedgehog	**U**	Umbrella Bird
I	Iguana	**V**	Vulture (Ruppell's)
J	Jerboa	**W**	Walrus
K	Koala	**X**	X-ray Fish (Pristella riddlei)
L	Lion	**Y**	Yak
M	Magpie (Pica pica) and Mole	**Z**	Zebra (chapman's)

for Corinna and Saskia

First published in the United States 1984 by Dial Books
A Division of NAL Penguin Inc.
2 Park Avenue
New York, New York 10016

Published in Great Britain by Lutterworth Press
Copyright © 1984 by Bert Kitchen
All rights reserved
Printed in Hong Kong by South China Printing Co.

OBE

6 8 10 9 7

Library of Congress Cataloging in Publication Data
Kitchen, Bert. Animal alphabet.
Summary: The reader is invited to guess the identity of twenty-six
unusual animals illustrating the letters of the alphabet.
1. English Language—Alphabet—Juvenile literature.
[1. Alphabet. 2. Animal. 3. Literary recreations.] I. Title
PE1155.K58 1984 [E] 83-23929
ISBN 0-8037-0117-9